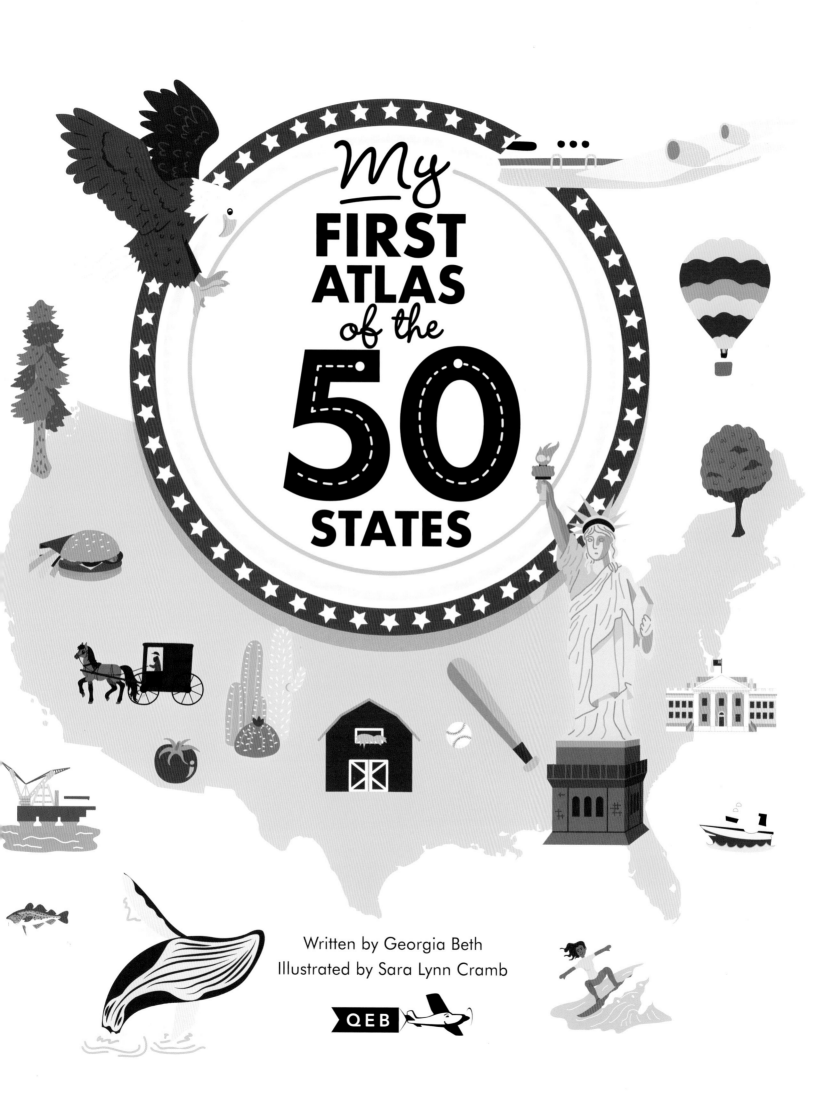

My
FIRST
ATLAS
of the
50
STATES

Written by Georgia Beth
Illustrated by Sara Lynn Cramb

QEB

Quarto is the authority on a wide range of topics.

Quarto educates, entertains and enriches the lives of our readers—enthusiasts and lovers of hands-on living.

www.quartoknows.com

Editor: Harriet Stone
Designer: Nick Leggett

© 2019 Quarto Publishing plc

This edition first published in 2019
by QEB Publishing,
an imprint of The Quarto Group.
6 Orchard Road, Suite 100
Lake Forest, CA 92630
T: +1 949 380 7510
F: +1 949 380 7575
www.QuartoKnows.com

A CIP record for this book is available from the Library of Congress.

ISBN 978 0 7112 4289 0

Manufactured in Shenzhen, China PP062019

9 8 7 6 5 4 3 2 1

Acknowledgements
The publisher thanks the following agencies for their kind permission to use their images.
Key: t=top, b=bottom, l=left, r=right, c=center

Shutterstock: 8tr Uwe Bergwitz; 8br youli zhao; 9tr Bill Draven; 9l Felix Nandzig; 9br Bill Draven; 10tl Mike Peters; 10bl blvdone; 10br Checubus; 11tr Jon Bilous; 11bl steve estvanik; 12tl Johnny Adolphson; 12tc S.Borisov; 13tr logoboom; 13c Javier Garcia; 13bl Uladzik Kryhin; 13br George Dolgikh; 14tl IM_photo;14c f11photo; 14br Matej Hudovernik; 15tl Tucker James; 15br CSNafzger; 16tl bjul; 16tr Johnny Adolphson; 16bl Jo Hunter; 17tl sumikophoto; 17cr Action Sports Photography; 18tl Timothy Yue; 18bl Anthony Ricci; 19bl Kris Wiktor; 20tr Sopotnicki; 20br Gray Photo Online; 21l neftali; 21br Galyna Andrushko; 22l William Silver; 22br Sean Pavone; 23tr Dean Fikar; 23rc Vivvi Smak; 23bl CrackerClips Stock Media; 24tr Life Atlas Photography; 24br Bogdan Denysyuk; 25tr Rich Koele; 25b Alex Pix; 26tc Everett Media; 26l Dane Jorgensen; 26bc Jim West/Alamy Stock Photo; 27br Sharon Day; 28tl Dorti; 28lc crotonoil; 28bc StockPhotoAstur; 29l Jeffrey J Coleman; 29r JB Manning; 30tr neal_johnson; 30br Malgorzata Litkowska; 31cl Eifel Kreutz; 31tr Joseph Sohm; 31br f11photo; 32c Svineyard; 32bc All Stock Photos; 33l f11photo; 33bc Ostranitsa Stanislav; 34tl Juli Hansen; 34bl John Panella; 35tl John McCormick; 35c Nagel Photography; 36tl anthony heflin; 36br MaxyM; 37tl Matteo Papetti; 37bc elesi; 38tr Action Sports Photogrpahy; 38cl Delmas Lehman; 39lc Thomas Kelley; 39rc Wangkun Jia; 39bl Irina Mos; 40tl anko70; 40bc Malgorzata Litkowska; 40cr jejim; 41tr Ferenc Szelepcsenyi; 41l Kevin Esterline; 42rc schusterbauer.com; 42bl BJ Ray; 43tr Checubus; 43c RIRF Stock; 43bc RosalreneBetancourt 7/Alamy Stock Photo; 44rc Jon Bilous; 45tl Andrew F. Kazmierski; 45l Bruce Ellis; 45bc Jon Bilous; 46tr Hale Kell; 46c Danita Delmont; 46bl Jill Lang; 47tr Sean Pavone; 47bl Sean Pavone; 47br Richard Ellis/Alamy Stock Photo; 48t Alan Falcony; 49cl Samot; 49cr Arto Hakola; 49bc NavinTar; 52t Joseph Sohm; 52l Jon Bilous; 52br Nicole S Glass; 53l EQRoy; 53tr Evertt Historical ESB Professional; 53br ESB Professional; 54t Mark Van Scyoc; 54bl Sean Pavone; 55tl mandritoiu; 55tr George Sheldon; 55br f11photo; 56tr mandritoiu; 56l Agnieszka Bacal; 57tr Salvan; 57cr Krasula; 57l vermontalm; 58tr sebastienlemyre; 58br Shackleford Photography; 59tl Salvan; 59c Racheal Grazias; 59br Wangkun Jia; 60l f11photo; 61tr Wangkun Jia; 61l Jose L Vilchez; 61br Joseph Sohm; 62cl CPQ; 62bc IM_photo; 63tr Aspen Photo; 63br Diego Grandi

Alamy:19cr imageBROKER/Alamy Stock Photo; 27l Joseph Sohm; 33tr David Lyons/Alamy Stock Photo; 35bc um West/Alamy; 37cr RGB Ventures/SuperStock/Alamy Stock Photo; 28br Peter Ptschelimzew/Alamy Stock Photo; 41br Matthew D. White/VWPics/Alamy; 44tr H. Mark Weidman Photography/Alamy Stock Photo; 44bl Cavan Images/Alamy Stock Photo; 50tr Jeff Greenberg/Alamy Stock Photo; 50l AB Forces News Collection/Alamy Stock Photo; 50br pr_camera; 51tr Pat & Chuck Blackley/Alamy; 51br Hemis/Alamy Stock Photo; 56rc Chase Guttman/Alamy Stock Photo; 60r Albert Knapp/Alamy Stock Photo; 60bc Randy Duchaine/Alamy Stock Photo; 62t debra millet/Alamy Stock;

Getty: 29t LawrenceSawyer; 30bl Tim Thompson; 48cl FrozenShutter; 51lc John Greim; 58l Daniel Joseph

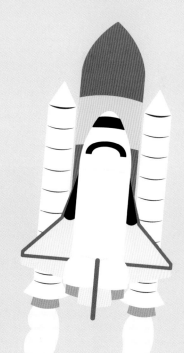

CONTENTS

WELCOME TO THE USA!

The United States of America was founded in 1776 and is now made up of 50 different states. The capital city is Washington, D.C. Located between Mexico and Canada, the U.S. is a big country—it's the fourth largest in the world!

ALASKA

UNITED STATES

HONOLULU

HAWAIIAN ISLANDS

HAWAI'I

KEY

Look for these in each state:

✳ STATE CAPITAL

● MAJOR CITY

ALASKA

CANADA

CANADA

WASHINGTON

OREGON

IDAHO

MONTANA

WYOMING

NEVADA

WELCOME TO Fabulous LAS VEGAS NEVADA

CALIFORNIA

UTAH

COLORADO

ARIZONA

NEW MEXICO

MEXICO

First States

Before the U.S. was created, native peoples lived on the land for many years. Then, in 1607, people arrived from England and settled in Jamestown, Virginia. They hoped to find a home where they could practice their religion. By 1776 there were 13 colonies, along the east coast.

On your journey through the atlas, look for icons that highlight each state's landmarks, animals, and more.

As you explore, look for fast facts about each state.

NORTH DAKOTA

SOUTH DAKOTA

MINNESOTA

WISCONSIN

NEBRASKA

IOWA

MICHIGAN

VERMONT

MAINE

NEW HAMPSHIRE
MASSACHUSETTS
RHODE ISLAND
CONNECTICUT

NEW YORK

PENNSYLVANIA

NEW JERSEY

DELAWARE
MARYLAND

ILLINOIS

INDIANA

OHIO

WEST VIRGINIA

VIRGINIA

KANSAS

MISSOURI

TENNESSEE

OKLAHOMA

ARKANSAS

KENTUCKY

NORTH CAROLINA

SOUTH CAROLINA

MISSISSIPPI

ALABAMA

GEORGIA

LOUISIANA

TEXAS

GULF OF MEXICO

FLORIDA

Diversity

Within the U.S.'s borders lies a great variety of landscapes and people. Over 320 million people live here. Some have come from other countries around the world.

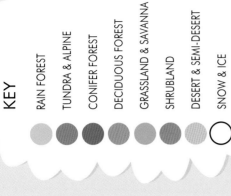

KEY

- RAIN FOREST
- TUNDRA & ALPINE
- CONIFER FOREST
- DECIDUOUS FOREST
- GRASSLAND & SAVANNA
- SHRUBLAND
- DESERT & SEMI-DESERT
- SNOW & ICE

NORTH AMERICA

The United States is part of North America. North America is a diverse continent, with a range of landscapes and climates. There are rain forests, deserts, mountains, prairies, and even snowy tundra. This map shows the different biomes across the continent and where they are found. The United States has a wide variety of biomes.

N

GREENLAND

CANADA

ALASKA
(UNITED STATES)

HAWAI'I
(UNITED STATES)

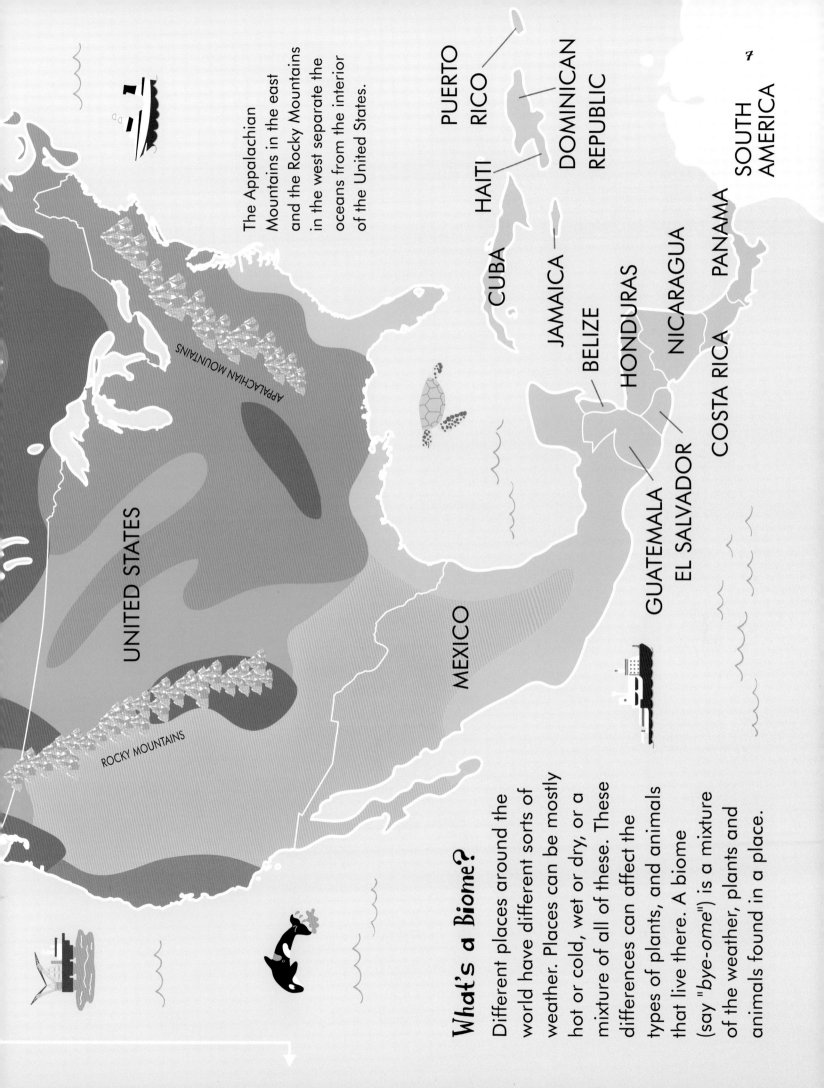

The Appalachian Mountains in the east and the Rocky Mountains in the west separate the oceans from the interior of the United States.

PUERTO RICO

DOMINICAN REPUBLIC

HAITI

CUBA

JAMAICA

BELIZE

HONDURAS

NICARAGUA

PANAMA

SOUTH AMERICA

GUATEMALA

EL SALVADOR

COSTA RICA

MEXICO

UNITED STATES

APPALACHIAN MOUNTAINS

ROCKY MOUNTAINS

What's a Biome?

Different places around the world have different sorts of weather. Places can be mostly hot or cold, wet or dry, or a mixture of all of these. These differences can affect the types of plants, and animals that live there. A biome (say "bye-ome") is a mixture of the weather, plants and animals found in a place.

ALASKA

Located in the northwest corner of North America, between Russia and Canada, Alaska is the largest state. There are beautiful mountains, glaciers, and valuable resources, but much of the land is icy tundra, and few people live here.

FAST FACTS

Size: 663,268 square miles (1,717,856 km²)

Population: 0.7 million

Joined the Union: January 3, 1959

State nickname: The Last Frontier

State bird: Willow ptarmigan

BEAUFORT SEA

N

shipping

grizzly bears

moose

dog sleds

BERING STRAIT

musk oxen

YUKON RIVER

KUSKOKWIM RIVER

FAIRBANKS

TANANA RIVER

wolves

Denali National Park

ANCHORAGE

CANADA

oil industry

black spruce

mining

JUNEAU

salmon

totem poles

bowhead whales

Denali National Park

Fly over Denali, formerly known as Mount McKinley, the highest peak in North America. It's home to wolves, moose, and grizzly bears.

Northern Lights

On special nights, stay up late to see the sky filled with beautiful green and blue lights.

PACIFIC OCEAN

HAWAI'I

In 1959, Hawai'i became the last state to join the Union. It's a group of eight islands in the Pacific Ocean formed from volcanoes that are still active today. The warm weather here makes Hawai'i a popular place for vacations.

Pineapple Garden Maze

Wind your way through the world's largest plant maze. There are more than 14,000 plants here!

KAUA'I

NI'IHAU

lei (flower garlands)

Pineapple Garden Maze

O'AHU

KAILUA

rainbows

PEARL HARBOR

HONOLULU

banana trees

Maunawili Falls

canoes

MOLOKA'I

LĀNA'I

LAHAINA

surfing

palm trees

KAHO'OLAWE

MAUI

Maunawili Falls

Hike up to the waterfall and take a dip in the cool pool water below.

Mauna Kea Observatory

Stargaze with these world-class telescopes. The clear, dark skies make this a popular place for astronomers to do research.

N

Mauna Kea Observatory

HAWAI'I

wild pigs

Hilo

volcanoes

humpback whales

FAST FACTS

Size: 10,970 square miles (28,412 km²)

Population: 1.4 million

Joined the Union: August 21, 1959

State nickname: Aloha State

State bird: Nene

Mount Rainier National Park

Wander through wildflowers and explore the forest that surrounds this active volcano.

WASHINGTON

Close to the Pacific Ocean, Canada, and Alaska, this state is important for trade in the U.S. There are many forests, fisheries, and farms. Most people live on the coast in Washington, where the weather is often rainy.

Olympic National Park

Space Needle

EVERETT

SEATTLE
BELLEVUE

coffee

TACOMA

OLYMPIA

CANADA

Chihuly Garden and Glass

COLVILLE RESERVATION

golden eagles

COLUMBIA RIVER

IDAHO

N

MONTANA

Grand Coulee Dam

SPOKANE

music industry

PACIFIC OCEAN

747 jets

Mount Rainier National Park

flannel shirts

rodeos

YAKAMA INDIAN RESERVATION

KENNEWICK

SNAKE RIVER

COLUMBIA RIVER

OREGON

Space Needle

Look out from the deck of this famous tower. The tilted glass windows are designed to give visitors amazing views of Seattle.

FAST FACTS

Size: 71,298 square miles (184,661 km^2)
Population: 7.5 million
Joined the Union: November 11, 1889
State nickname: Evergreen State
State bird: American goldfinch

Chihuly Garden and Glass

Tour the work of sculptor Dale Chihuly. A team of artists will show you his glassblowing style.

OREGON

Oregon is a diverse state. There are rain forests, mountains, valleys, deserts, and beaches. The forests provide many jobs, as do the farms and cities in the Willamette River Valley, where most of the people live.

N

FAST FACTS

Size: 98,379 square miles (254,800 km²)
Population: 4.2 million
Joined the Union: February 14, 1859
State nickname: Beaver State
State bird: Western meadowlark

Oregon Trail

Travel back in time with a visit to the Oregon Trail. It was used by trappers, traders, religious preachers, and settlers as they moved west in the 1800s.

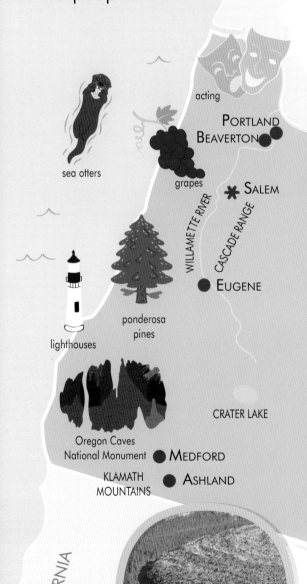

sea otters

acting

grapes

PORTLAND
BEAVERTON

*SALEM

WILLAMETTE RIVER

CASCADE RANGE

Multnomah Falls

WASHINGTON

COLUMBIA RIVER

ponderosa pines

lighthouses

● EUGENE

BEND ●

Moon country

Oregon Trail

Hells Canyon

SNAKE RIVER

Oregon Caves National Monument ● MEDFORD

KLAMATH MOUNTAINS ● ASHLAND

CRATER LAKE

elk

beavers

IDAHO

CALIFORNIA

Moon Country

Explore central Oregon's lava fields. Astronauts trained to walk on the Moon here.

NEVADA

CALIFORNIA

California is home to more people than any other state. Most people live in the cities. There are also deserts, mountains, beaches, and many farms too. The food grown in California is eaten all across the U.S.

Mount Whitney

Climb one of the highest mountains in the country. It is part of the Sierra Nevada mountains.

OREGON

FAST FACTS

Size: 163,695 square miles (423,968 km^2)

Population: 39 million

Joined the Union: September 9, 1850

State nickname: Golden State

State bird: California quail

Mojave Desert

Watch the sunset over the sand dunes. This is the driest desert in the country.

N

SHASTA RIVER

SACRAMENTO RIVER

redwood forest

whales

Napa Valley

dairy farming

avocado farming

bald eagles

SACRAMENTO

Yosemite National Park

Golden Gate Bridge

Silicon Valley

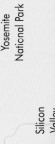

SAN FRANCISCO

sea otters

NEVADA

ARIZONA

MEXICO

COLORADO RIVER

DEATH VALLEY

MOJAVE DESERT

joshua trees

tacos

Mission Basilica

cacti

Mount Whitney

quails

HOLLYWOOD
Hollywood

• Los Angeles

San Joaquin River

bears

palm trees

almonds

orange farming

sea lions

San Diego •

PACIFIC OCEAN

Hollywood

Home of the world's leading movie companies, and where many famous actors live in grand houses.

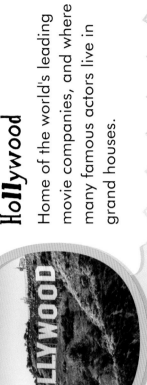

Silicon Valley

Visit a maker space or design an app. Silicon Valley is home to big tech companies like Apple.

Pacific Ocean

Surf, swim, or play a game of volleyball at the beach. The coastline stretches over 1,000 miles (1,600 km).

Tacos

Eat a round of tacos. Mexican cuisine is a favorite here.

NEVADA

The name Nevada means "snow clad," but most of this large state is a desert. It began as a place to mine silver. Today most people who live here work in Las Vegas. Over 40 million people visit Las Vegas each year.

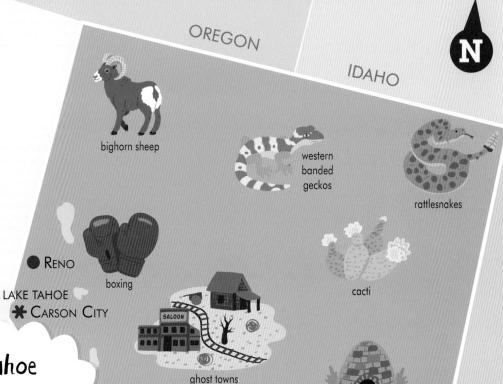

OREGON

IDAHO

bighorn sheep

western banded geckos

rattlesnakes

● RENO

boxing

cacti

LAKE TAHOE

✻ CARSON CITY

SALOON

ghost towns

beehive charcoal ovens

UTAH

sagebrush

mining

WELCOME to Fabulous LAS VEGAS NEVADA

Las Vegas

petroglyphs

LAS VEGAS

ARIZONA

Hoover Dam

CALIFORNIA

Lake Tahoe

Relax at Lake Tahoe. Surrounded by mountains and trees, it is known for its clear water.

Las Vegas

Watch a concert or see a show. Some of the world's best musicians, dancers, and singers perform here.

FAST FACTS

Size: 110,572 square miles (286,380 km²)

Population: 3 million

Joined the Union: October 31, 1864

State nickname: Silver State

State bird: Mountain bluebird

The Hoover Dam

Tour the Hoover Dam. It produces power for California, Nevada, and Arizona.

PACIFIC OCEAN

14

IDAHO

The name Idaho comes from a Native American Shoshone phrase that means "Gem of the Mountains." The outline of this state looks like a boot. Logging and mining are important industries here, but many areas are still wild, with no roads or settlers.

CANADA

Craters of the Moon National Monument

Visit a field of extinct volcanoes. Cones, craters, and lava flows make this area look like the surface of the Moon.

square dancing

● COEUR D'ALENE

logging

Idaho giant salamanders

N

OREGON

peregrine falcons

golf

MONTANA

FAST FACTS

Size: 83,569 square miles (216,443 km²)

Population: 1.7 million

Joined the Union: July 3, 1890

State nickname: Gem State

State bird: Mountain bluebird

CALDWELL ● MERIDIAN
NAMPA ●●✳ BOISE

Sun Valley

fishing

IDAHO FALLS ●

Craters of the Moon National Monument

hot springs

POCATELLO ●

SNAKE RIVER

cutthroat trout

potatoes

BEAR RIVER

Sun Valley

Snowboard, ski, or snowshoe in Sun Valley. This area is famous for its winter sports.

NEVADA

UTAH

WYOMING

15

UTAH

In 1847 Utah was settled by people looking for religious freedom. Today it is home to the headquarters of the Mormon Church. Nearly 70 percent of people who live in Utah today are Mormons.

FAST FACTS

Size: 84,898 square miles (219,885 km²)
Population: 3.1 million
Joined the Union: January 4, 1896
State nickname: Beehive State
State bird: California gull

Zion National Park

Admire the colorful canyons and dramatic cliffs.

blue spruce

cherries

OGDEN

GREAT SALT LAKE

BONNEVILLE SALT FLATS

Mormon Tabernacle

WEST VALLEY CITY

SALT LAKE CITY

WEST JORDAN

SANDY

OREM

PROVO

covered wagons

beehives

WYOMING

GREEN RIVER

Dutch ovens

bison

FISHLAKE NATIONAL FOREST

NEVADA

N

Rocky Mountain elk

Bryce Canyon

mule deer

Arches

Mormon Tabernacle

Listen to the world-famous choir sing with an organ that has over 11,000 pipes.

Zion National Park

GRAND STAIRCASE-ESCALANTE NATIONAL MONUMENT

LAKE POWELL

aspens

COLORADO PLATEAU

COLORADO

Four Corners

Stand in four states at once where the borders of Colorado, Arizona, New Mexico, and Utah all join together.

ARIZONA

NEW MEXICO

The Grand Canyon

Ride a donkey, river raft, or hike through the Grand Canyon. Visitors agree it is one of the most beautiful places on Earth.

FAST FACTS

Size: 113,990 square miles (295,233 km²)
Population: 7 million
Joined the Union: February 14, 1912
State nickname: Grand Canyon State
State bird: Cactus wren

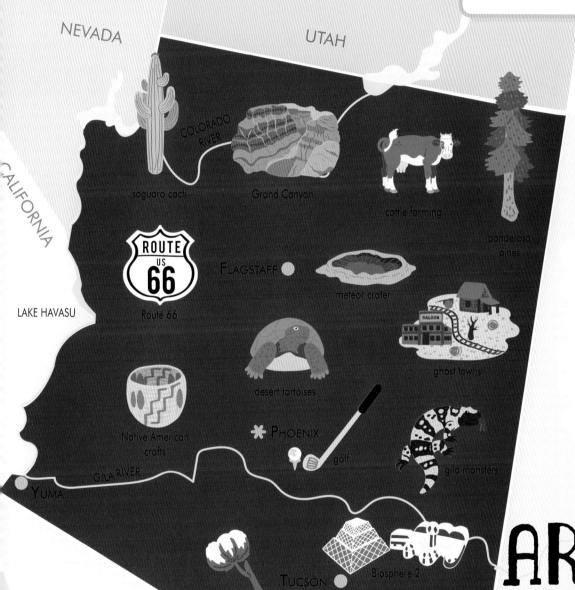

NEVADA

UTAH

CALIFORNIA

COLORADO RIVER

saguaro cacti

Grand Canyon

cattle farming

ponderosa pines

ROUTE US 66

FLAGSTAFF

meteor crater

LAKE HAVASU

Route 66

SALOON

ghost towns

desert tortoises

Native American crafts

PHOENIX

golf

gila monsters

GILA RIVER

YUMA

Biosphere 2

TUCSON

cotton farming

MEXICO

N

GULF OF CALIFORNIA

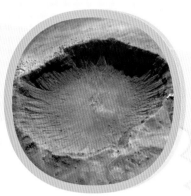

Meteor Crater

See where a meteorite hit 50,000 years ago. The crater is nearly a mile across.

ARIZONA

Known for hot weather and beautiful deserts, Arizona is a favorite place to vacation. There are unusual animals and ancient monuments. And no visit is complete without a trip to the Grand Canyon.

MONTANA

Montana is one of the largest states in the U.S., but only two states have fewer people living in them. The western side of the state is part of the Rocky Mountains. The eastern side is part of the Great Plains. Montana's official state animal is the grizzly bear.

Skiing

Ski downhill or cross country in a ski resort. Lone Mountain, at over 11,160 feet tall is a popular peak for skiing.

grizzly bears

coal mining

ponderosa pines

bison

GREAT FALLS

MISSOURI RIVER

● MISSOULA

Angus cattle

gold mining

✳ HELENA

huckleberries

FORT PECK LAKE

fishing

skiing

cowboys

dinosaur fossils

BOZEMAN ●

sheep farming

BILLINGS ●

YELLOWSTONE RIVER

Yellowstone National Park

horses

N

CANADA

IDAHO

WYOMING

UTAH

NORTH DAKOTA

Riding

Take in big sky country on horseback. Or hike with a llama! It's easier to enjoy the view when they're carrying your gear.

FAST FACTS

Size: 147,040 square miles (380,832 km^2)

Population: 1 million

Joined the Union: November 8, 1889

State nickname: Treasure State or Big Sky Country

State bird: Western meadowlark

WYOMING

Surrounded by other states, Wyoming is known for its vast, open plains, with roaming wildlife. There are almost as many pronghorn living in Wyoming as people. Devil's Tower was the first national monument in the United States.

NORTH DAKOTA

MONTANA

N

IDAHO

SOUTH DAKOTA

Yellowstone National Park

CODY

Grand Teton National Park

black bears

mule deer

Devil's Tower

JACKSON

ROCKY MOUNTAINS

BIGHORN RIVER

elk

wolves

THE GREAT PLAINS

CASPER

pronghorn

rodeos

NORTH PLATTE RIVER

UTAH

Fossil Butte National Monument

sheep farming

sagebrush

CHEYENNE

COLORADO

Yellowstone National Park

Watch the geysers spout and see mudpots and colorful hot springs in America's first national park.

Fossil Butte National Monument

Study the largest collection of freshwater fish fossils in the world. This area used to be a large lake where these fish once swam.

COLORADO

Made up of plains and mountains, much of Colorado is dry. The landscape is broken up by abandoned towns, known as ghost towns, from America's early frontier days. Today most people live in a hilly landscape known as the Colorado Piedmont.

Mesa Verde National Park

Tour the remains of cliff-dwellings built by Native Americans. It is now a World Heritage site.

WYOMING

UTAH

bighorn sheep

Rocky Mountain National Park

FORT COLLINS

COLORADO PIEDMONT

BOULDER

THORNTON

WESTMINSTER

DENVER

LAKEWOOD

AURORA

mountain goats

COLORADO RIVER

ASPEN

lark buntings

NEBRASKA

KANSAS

western tiger salamanders

skiing

Garden of the Gods

COLORADO SPRINGS

jackrabbits

prairie dogs

TELLURIDE

PUEBLO

ARKANSAS RIVER

Mesa Verde National Park

coyotes

RIO GRANDE

GREAT SAND DUNES NATIONAL MONUMENT

claret cup cacti

juniper trees

NEW MEXICO

N

FAST FACTS

Size: 104,094 square miles (269,602 km^2)

Population: 5.6 million

Joined the Union: August 1, 1876

State nickname: Centennial State

State bird: Lark bunting

Garden of the Gods

Go rock climbing in a dramatic red landscape. Then visit the museum to learn how the rocks were formed.

NEW MEXICO

This state used to belong to Spain and then Mexico. The cultures of the two countries can still be felt here. Native Americans, ranchers, cowboys, and miners have also played a role in the state's history.

Size: 121,590 square miles (314,917 km²)

Population: 2 million

Joined the Union: January 6, 1912

State nickname: Land of Enchantment

State bird: Roadrunner

COLORADO

● FARMINGTON

Navajo blankets

Georgia O'Keeffe house

Wheeler Peak

● TAOS

CAPULIN VOLCANO NATIONAL MONUMENT

Los Alamos National Laboratory

SANTA FE

SANTA FE TRAIL

ARIZONA

covered wagons

roadrunners

ALBUQUERQUE ●

trains

CANADIAN RIVER

N

coyotes

PECOS RIVER

hot air balloons

UFOs

RIO GRANDE RIVER

Gila cliff dwellings

yuccas

WHITE SANDS NATIONAL MONUMENT

ROSWELL ●

cacti

● LAS CRUCES

Carlsbad Caverns

chili peppers

MEXICO

TEXAS

Georgia O'Keeffe House

Visit the home where artist Georgia O'Keeffe worked, and see the landscape that inspired her most famous paintings.

Carlsbad Caverns

Go underground to see some of the world's largest rock formations. They were formed when acid rain dissolved the limestone.

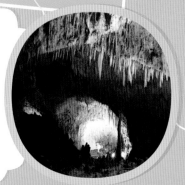

TEXAS

The second largest state in the country, Texas is nearly 1,000 miles (1,600 km) across. The western side is dryer than the east, and is known for ranching. Texas produces more oil than any other state in the U.S.—over 4 million barrels per day.

ranching

CANADIAN RIVER

angus cattle

cowboys

NEW MEXICO

● EL PASO

GUADALUPE PEAK

prickly pear cacti

cotton farming

PECOS RIVER

armadillos

Big Bend National Park

Go bird watching and wander through a meadow of cactus flowers. There are canyons, deserts, mountains, and the Rio Grande river in this national park.

N

MEXICO

Big Bend National Park

RIO GRANDE RIVER

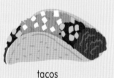
tacos

tumbleweed

San Antonio River Walk

Take a water taxi along the river. Stop to listen to some live music and explore a historic Christian mission building. Then eat in one of the many TexMex restaurants here.

FAST FACTS

Size: 268,597 square miles (695,663 km²)

Population: 28 million

Joined the Union: December 29, 1845

State nickname: Lone Star State

State bird: Northern mockingbird

OKLAHOMA

ARKANSAS

RED RIVER

fiddles

FORT ● ● DALLAS
WORTH

coral snakes

oil wells

BRAZOS RIVER

✳ AUSTIN

Alamo Mission

N
NTONIO

SAN ANTONIO RIVER

HOUSTON

NASA's Johnson Space Center ●

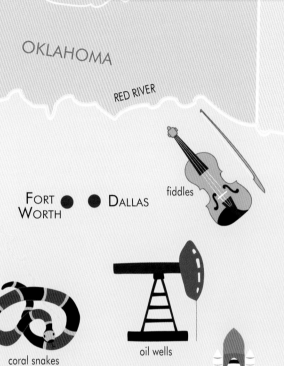

pinatas

GULF OF MEXICO

PADRE ISLAND

Alamo Mission

Visit the mission in San Antonio that was home to the famous Battle of the Alamo, where Texans fought for independence from Mexico. You might even see a reenactment.

LOUISIANA

NASA's Johnson Space Center

Tour the control center for the International Space Station and learn how humans landed on the Moon. This is where astronauts train before heading into space.

Padre Island National Seashore

Fish, build a sand castle, or go sailing. The water here is even saltier than the ocean!

NORTH DAKOTA

North Dakota has a history of fur trading and hunting. Today it is home to many farms and ranches but few people. Across the state, temperatures can reach as high as 120°F (49°C) and as low as -60°F (-51°C). The town of Rugby is the geographic center of North America.

International Peace Garden

Located on the Canadian border, this park is a good place to camp, bird watch, and enjoy the beautiful flowers that are planted here.

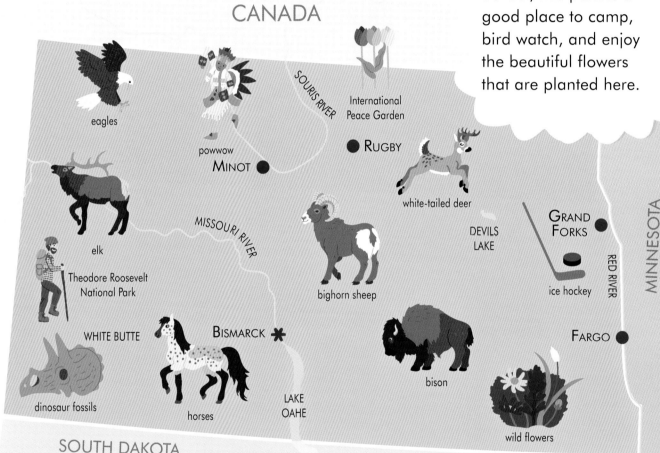

CANADA

eagles

powwow

MINOT

SOURIS RIVER

International Peace Garden

RUGBY

white-tailed deer

elk

MISSOURI RIVER

bighorn sheep

DEVILS LAKE

GRAND FORKS

ice hockey

RED RIVER

Theodore Roosevelt National Park

WHITE BUTTE

BISMARCK

dinosaur fossils

horses

LAKE OAHE

bison

FARGO

wild flowers

MONTANA

MINNESOTA

SOUTH DAKOTA

Maah Daah Hey Trail

Bike ride through Theodore Roosevelt National Park and see eagles, bison, and bighorn sheep. The name Maah Daah Hey means "an area that will be around for a long time."

SOUTH DAKOTA

Found in the center of the United States, South Dakota is a rural state known for its large plains. The city of Pierre is one of the smallest state capitals. South Dakota's stunning Badlands National Park was established in 1939.

The Mammoth Site

Visit Hot Springs to watch an active archeological dig. Mammoth bones and fossils from Ice Age creatures have been uncovered here.

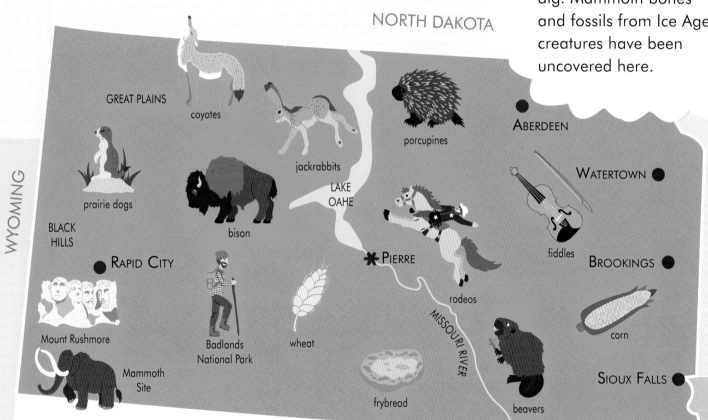

NORTH DAKOTA

GREAT PLAINS

coyotes

porcupines

ABERDEEN

jackrabbits

WATERTOWN

LAKE OAHE

WYOMING

prairie dogs

BLACK HILLS

bison

fiddles

RAPID CITY

PIERRE

BROOKINGS

rodeos

Mount Rushmore

Badlands National Park

wheat

MISSOURI RIVER

corn

MINNESOTA

Mammoth Site

frybread

beavers

SIOUX FALLS

NEBRASKA

FAST FACTS

Size: 77,116 square miles (199,730 km²)

Population: 0.9 million

Joined the Union: November 2, 1889

State nickname: The Mount Rushmore State

State bird: Ring-necked pheasant

Mount Rushmore National Memorial

Admire the faces of George Washington, Thomas Jefferson, Theodore Roosevelt, and Abraham Lincoln, and learn how they transformed the nation. This iconic monument was carved between 1927 and 1941.

NEBRASKA

As part of the Midwest, Nebraska was a popular place for trappers, miners, and other people to stop while traveling from across the U.S. Today the state produces a lot of the country's food, especially meat and corn. It is also known for its huge grasslands.

FAST FACTS

Size: 77,347 square miles (200,328 km²)
Population: 1.9 million
Joined the Union: March 1, 1867
State nickname: Cornhusker State
State bird: Western meadowlark

The Archway

Learn about the people who traveled along the Platte River Road. This museum is a tribute to the nation's first coast-to-coast highway.

SOUTH DAKOTA

WYOMING

Sandhill crane

SAND HILLS

prairie dogs

SCOTTSBLUFF

NORTH PLATTE RIVER

catfish

bison

GREAT PLAINS

windmills

square dancing

Ashfall Fossil Beds State Historical Park

MISSOURI RIVER

IOWA

Henry Doorly Zoo

NORTH PLATTE

GRAND ISLAND

PLATTE RIVER

OMAHA

KEARNEY

LINCOLN ✳

canoeing

goldenrod

The Archway

KANSAS

Henry Doorly Zoo

Get up close with Nebraska's most exotic residents. One of the best in the country, this zoo has many animals, including orangutans, penguins, and sharks.

Ashfall Fossil Beds State Historical Park

Visit the site of an ancient volcano that's now a fascinating fossil bed. Watch as paleontologists uncover barrel-bodied rhinos, camels, and other creatures.

KANSAS

The name Kansas comes from a Siouan phrase meaning "people of the south wind." The state is known for tornadoes and windy weather. Nearly 90 percent of the land is used for farming. Much of the country's airplane production is done here, too.

FAST FACTS

Size: 82,278 square miles (213,099 km²)
Population: 3 million
Joined the Union: January 29, 1861
State nickname: Sunflower State
State bird: Western meadowlark

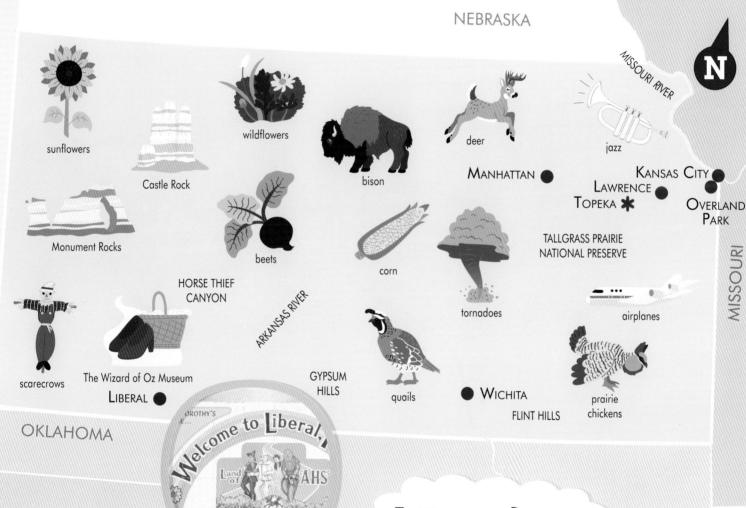

NEBRASKA

COLORADO

MISSOURI RIVER

N

sunflowers

Castle Rock

Monument Rocks

wildflowers

beets

HORSE THIEF CANYON

bison

corn

ARKANSAS RIVER

deer

jazz

MANHATTAN

KANSAS CITY
LAWRENCE
TOPEKA
OVERLAND PARK

TALLGRASS PRAIRIE NATIONAL PRESERVE

tornadoes

airplanes

MISSOURI

scarecrows

The Wizard of Oz Museum

LIBERAL

OKLAHOMA

GYPSUM HILLS

quails

WICHITA
FLINT HILLS

prairie chickens

Welcome to Liberal,
DOROTHY'S ...E...
Land of ...AHS

The Wizard of Oz Museum

Check out memorabilia about this classic film, book, and stage show. Then visit Liberal to see a replica of Dorothy's house.

Tallgrass Prairie National Preserve

See how the prairie looked when settlers first arrived. There are 11,000 acres and several historic buildings to explore here.

OKLAHOMA

The state of Oklahoma bridges Northern and Southern culture in America. The land is varied, with mountains, plains, grasslands, and forests. The Red Earth Festival, celebrating Native American cultures, is held in Oklahoma every year.

Will Rogers Memorial

Learn about celebrity cowboy Will Rogers at this museum. There's memorabilia, plus art, a library, and a theater.

KANSAS

ARKANSAS

NEW MEXICO

OZARK PLATEAU

basketball

TULSA

Will Rogers Memorial Museum

STILLWATER

ARKANSAS RIVER

ROUTE US 66

cotton farming

EDMOND

CANADIAN RIVER

OKLAHOMA CITY
NORMAN

prairie dogs

Route 66 Museum

oil wells

bison

GYPSUM HILLS

CHICKASAW NATIONAL RECREATION AREA

wheat

LAWTON

cacti

tornadoes

RED RIVER

TEXAS

N

Chickasaw National Recreation Area

Swim, boat, or fish in the waterfalls, streams, and swimming holes of this beautiful park.

The Oklahoma Route 66 Museum

Study the history of America's famous cross-country highway. The exhibits will help you understand what America used to be like. You can even sit at the counter of a 1950s diner.

Forestville Mystery Cave State Park

Learn about pioneer life in the 1800s in this preserved town. Then tour the state's longest cave.

MINNESOTA

Minnesota has over 10,000 lakes and is home to large forests and prairies. The state is known for its extreme winters. Minneapolis is one of the more modern cities in the Midwest. There are lots of new restaurants and homes, as well as art museums, sports teams, and businesses.

NORTH DAKOTA

Mall of America

Wander through over 500 stores at the biggest mall in the United States. There's also an aquarium, a roller coaster, and a butterfly garden.

pine trees

foxes

RED LAKE

loons

CANADA

Boundary Waters

LAKE SUPERIOR

RED RIVER

logging

LAKE WINNIBIGOSHISH

ST. LOUIS RIVER

walleye fish

DULUTH

GM crops

turkeys

MISSISSIPPI RIVER

MILLE LACS LAKE

deer

beavers

WISCONSIN

ST. CLOUD

MINNEAPOLIS   ST. PAUL

BLOOMINGTON   EAGAN

Mall of America

MANKATO

Forestville Mystery Cave State Park

SOUTH DAKOTA

FAST FACTS

Size: 86,935 square miles (225,161 km²)

Population: 5.6 million

Joined the Union: May 11, 1858

State nickname: North Star State

State bird: Common loon

IOWA

N

Boundary Waters

Canoe from lake to lake in the northeastern tip of the state. You may even spot a majestic bald eagle flying above you.

IOWA

This Midwestern state is mostly farmland. People here live far apart, and cities are small. Every four years, Iowa plays a large role in the presidential election when it holds the first caucuses, or meetings, to discuss the candidates.

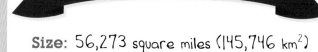

Size: 56,273 square miles (145,746 km²)
Population: 3 million
Joined the Union: December 28, 1846
State nickname: Hawkeye State
State bird: Eastern goldfinch

WISCONSIN

MINNESOTA

MISSISSIPPI RIVER

bald eagles

SIOUX CITY

elm trees

farming

deer

MISSOURI RIVER

NEBRASKA

chickens

ballots

John and Mary Pappajohn
Sculpture Park

CEDAR RAPIDS

squirrels

DAVENPORT

DES MOINES

PELLA

trout

covered bridges of
Madison County

tulips

otters

ILLINOIS

MISSOURI

Tulip Time Festival

Stop to smell the flowers at the annual tulip festival in Pella. The town was founded by immigrants from Holland.

John and Mary Pappajohn Sculpture Park

Admire this large collection of sculptures in downtown Des Moines. It looks especially impressive at night.

The Bridges of Madison County

Travel under one of Wisconsin's famous covered bridges. They date back to the 1880s.

MISSOURI

The eastern forests, western prairies, southern cotton fields, and northern cornfields all meet in Missouri. For those who live in the east, Missouri is known as the gateway to the west. Gateway Arch National Park contains the tallest arch in the world.

Mark Twain in Hannibal

See author Mark Twain's childhood home and the town of Hannibal, which inspired his books *The Adventures of Tom Sawyer* and *The Adventures of Huckleberry Finn*.

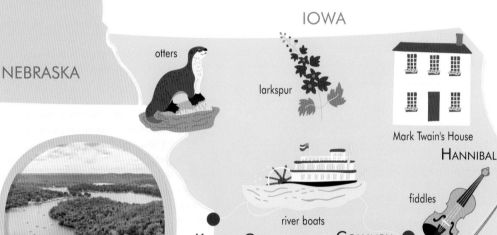

IOWA

NEBRASKA

otters

larkspur

Mark Twain's House

HANNIBAL

MISSISSIPPI RIVER

river boats

fiddles

KANSAS CITY

COLUMBIA

Gateway Arch

JEFFERSON CITY

MISSOURI RIVER

ST. LOUIS

ILLINOIS

KANSAS

LAKE OF THE OZARKS

elk

turkeys

Taum Sauk Mountain

Lake of the Ozarks

Spend a day fishing on Missouri's largest lake, then take in the colorful sunset.

SPRINGFIELD

JOPLIN

OZARKS

corn

BRANSON

farming

KENTUCKY

ARKANSAS

TENNESSEE

FAST FACTS

Size: 69,707 square miles (180,540 km²)

Population: 6 million

Joined the Union: August 10, 1821

State nickname: Show Me State

State bird: Eastern bluebird

The Gateway Arch

Ride up inside this famous monument. At the top you can enjoy a panoramic view of St. Louis.

ARKANSAS

Arkansas is a small state in the south. It includes the Ozark mountains, farmland, and a number of rivers. More than half the state is forest. The fiddle is Arkansas' state musical instrument.

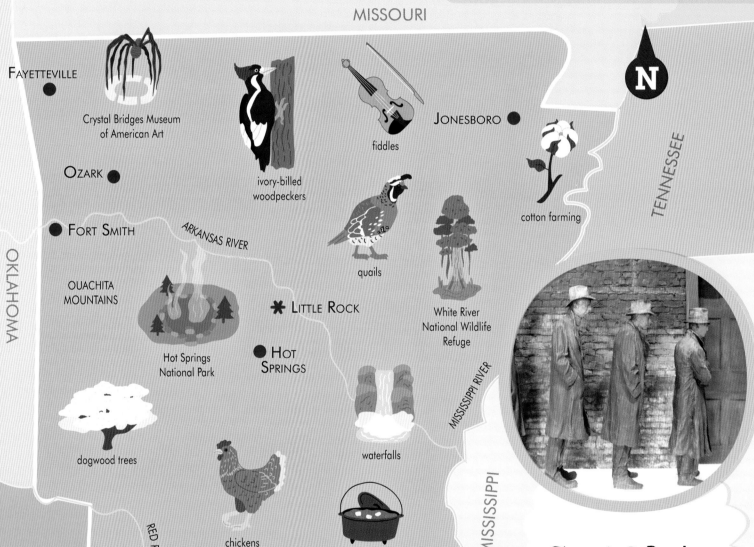

MISSOURI

FAYETTEVILLE

Crystal Bridges Museum of American Art

OZARK

FORT SMITH

ARKANSAS RIVER

OKLAHOMA

OUACHITA MOUNTAINS

Hot Springs National Park

ivory-billed woodpeckers

fiddles

JONESBORO

cotton farming

TENNESSEE

N

quails

LITTLE ROCK

HOT SPRINGS

White River National Wildlife Refuge

MISSISSIPPI RIVER

dogwood trees

chickens

Dutch oven

waterfalls

MISSISSIPPI

RED RIVER

Crystal Bridges Museum of American Art

Tour this world-class modern art museum, then enjoy the nature trails outside.

Hot Springs National Park

Enjoy one of the 47 thermal springs in this park. You can hike, taste the water, or picnic here.

LOUISIANA

This state was part of the Louisiana Purchase which helped to double the size of the country. Firmly in the south, it has a subtropical climate and the soil is very fertile. Louisiana was named by French explorers after King Louis XIV of France.

FAST FACTS

Size: 52,375 square miles (135,651 km²)
Population: 4.7 million
Joined the Union: April 30, 1812
State nickname: Pelican State
State bird: Eastern brown pelican

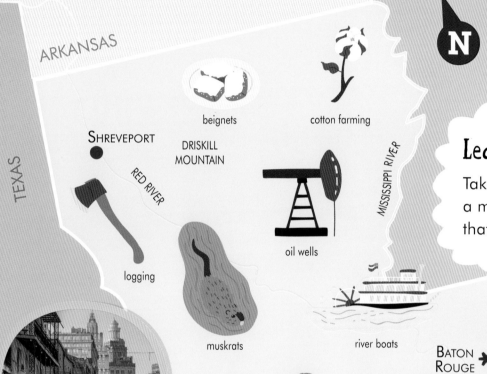

ARKANSAS

MISSISSIPPI

N

TEXAS

SHREVEPORT

beignets

cotton farming

DRISKILL MOUNTAIN

RED RIVER

MISSISSIPPI RIVER

oil wells

logging

muskrats

river boats

Learn Creole

Take a class to learn some Creole, a mix of French and African words that is distinct to the region.

BATON ROUGE

LAFAYETTE

METAIRIE
NEW ORLEANS

jazz

LAKE CHARLES

bald cypress tree

alligators

GULF OF MEXICO

French Quarter

Listen to some of the best jazz musicians in the world, then get your fortune told by a tarot card reader in New Orleans.

Louisiana Food

Feast on a po' boy sandwich, dig into a bowl of jambalaya, or try a sweet beignet. Louisiana is the birthplace of many famous, tasty foods.

Taliesin

Tour the house where architect Frank Lloyd Wright worked, in Spring Green.

WISCONSIN

Located in the north, Wisconsin is known for its cold winters. It produces more cheese than any other state, and also makes lots of milk and butter. Like its neighbor Minnesota, Wisconsin has over 10,000 lakes. The forests in the north are a popular place to vacation.

APOSTLE ISLANDS

LAKE SUPERIOR

MICHIGAN

BRULE RIVER

MENOMINEE RIVER

farming

MINNESOTA

WISCONSIN RIVER

maple trees

corn

Swiss cheese

DOOR PENINSULA

dairy cows

Amish buggy

GREEN BAY

APPLETON

LAKE WINNEBAGO

LAKE MICHIGAN

N

MISSISSIPPI RIVER

balsam firs

badgers

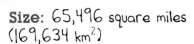
FAST FACTS

Size: 65,496 square miles (169,634 km^2)

Population: 5.8 million

Joined the Union: May 29, 1848

State nickname: Badger State

State bird: American robin

Taliesin

WAUKESHA

●● MILWAUKEE

white tailed deer

SPRING GREEN

Football

RACINE ●

KENOSHA ●

IOWA

Amish Communities

Visit the Amish towns that are spread across the state. Admire their woodworking and taste their delicious baked goods.

ILLINOIS

Sleeping Bear Dunes National Park

Climb the sand dunes, canoe, bike, or hike. There are scenic outlooks all around this beautiful park.

MICHIGAN

CANADA

Michigan is a northern state that's bordered by four lakes: Lake Erie, Lake Huron, Lake Superior, and Lake Michigan. Much of the land is flat and wooded, and the state is split into two pieces. The Upper Peninsula has many resources but few people. Most people live in the mitten-shaped Lower Peninsula.

LAKE SUPERIOR

UPPER PENINSULA

STRAITS OF MACKINAC

N

beavers

oak trees

Mackinac Bridge

LOWER PENINSULA

LAKE HURON

WISCONSIN

boating

SLEEPING BEAR DUNES NATIONAL LAKESHORE

AU SABLE RIVER

cherries

Motown Records

CASS RIVER

CANADA

SAGINAW

FLINT

Mackinac Bridge

Drive across the bridge that connects the Upper and Lower Peninsulas. You can also visit Mackinac Island, where people can ride bikes, but not drive, because cars are not allowed on the island.

GRAND RAPIDS

LANSING

car manufacturing

GRAND RIVER

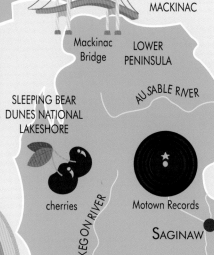

MUSKEGON RIVER

ANN ARBOR

DETROIT

windmill

KALAMAZOO

LAKE ERIE

American Center for Mobility

OHIO

LAKE MICHIGAN

INDIANA

FAST FACTS

Size: 96,713 square miles (250,486 km²)

Population: 10 million

Joined the Union: January 26, 1837

State nickname: Great Lakes State

State bird: American robin

American Center for Mobility

Check out the new self-driving cars in Detroit, the city where the technology started. Detroit is famous for manufacturing cars.

ILLINOIS

The midwestern state of Illinois is home to Chicago, one of the biggest cities in the country and the starting place of the famous Route 66 highway. The south of the state is rural, home to many farms. Illinois' state mammal is the white-tailed deer.

LAKE MICHIGAN

N

WISCONSIN

Garden of the Gods

Take a picture in one of the most photographed places in the state. This area of the Shawnee National Forest is famous for its sandstone rock formations.

INDIANA

Art Institute of Chicago

CHICAGO

Millennium Park

MIDEWIN NATIONAL TALLGRASS PRAIRIE

KANKAKEE RIVER

JOLIET

Fermi Laboratory

DES PLAINES RIVER

farming

CHAMPAIGN

URBANA

DECATUR

trains

corn

yellow bass

NORMAL

BLOOMINGTON

CHARLES MOUND

PEORIA

Lincoln Home National Historic Site

SPRINGFIELD

oak trees

ILLINOIS RIVER

IOWA

Art Institute of Chicago

See the masterpieces on display at this famous museum. Then walk across the street to admire Lake Michigan.

Lincoln Home National Historic Site

Tour President Abraham Lincoln's home in Springfield. The rooms have been restored to look the way they did in 1860.

KENTUCKY

Fermi National Accelerator Laboratory

Visit this world-class laboratory and ask a scientist anything you've ever wanted to know about physics. The scientists here are studying how the universe works.

apples

hickory trees

OHIO RIVER
Garden of the Gods

SHAWNEE NATIONAL FOREST

porcupines

coal mining

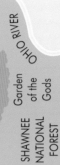
white-tailed deer

MISSOURI

...SSIPPI RIVER

Millennium Park

Explore the Chicago lakefront. There's a Ferris Wheel, a skating rink, and a theater in this park.

FAST FACTS

Size: 57,914 square miles (149,997 km²)

Population: 13 million

Joined the Union: December 3, 1818

State nickname: Prairie State

State bird: Northern cardinal

INDIANA

As its motto says, Indiana lies "at the crossroads of America." This small Midwestern state is home to many factories and farms. The name Indiana means "Land of the Indians."

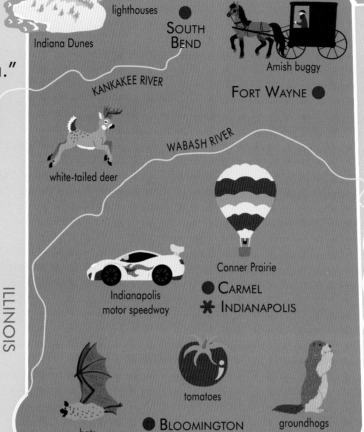

MICHIGAN

lighthouses
Indiana Dunes
SOUTH BEND
Amish buggy
FORT WAYNE

KANKAKEE RIVER

WABASH RIVER

white-tailed deer

ILLINOIS

Conner Prairie
CARMEL
Indianapolis motor speedway
* INDIANAPOLIS

tomatoes
bats
BLOOMINGTON
groundhogs

OHIO

Sandhill cranes
OHIO RIVER

hickory trees

EVANSVILLE

KENTUCKY

Indiana Dunes

Hike the trails or swim in Lake Michigan. These sand dunes can be nearly 200 feet (61 m) tall.

Indianapolis Motor Speedway

Watch cars race around this famous track at the Indy 500. The race happens every year on Memorial Day weekend in May.

Conner Prairie

Travel back in time to 1836. This living history park shows what life was like on Indiana's first farms. You can also take a hot air balloon ride over the state.

N

FAST FACTS

Size: 36,420 square miles (94,327 km²)
Population: 7 million
Joined the Union: December 11, 1816
State nickname: Hoosier State
State bird: Northern cardinal

KENTUCKY

This southern state is home to Bluegrass prairies, sinkholes, caves, and mountains. Many important battles in the Civil War (1861-1865) were fought here. Today most of the state is rural and covered with small towns.

Churchill Downs Track

Wear a fancy hat and join in the fun at the Kentucky Derby. This race track is famous for its annual horse race.

OHIO

APPALACHIAN MOUNTAINS

WEST VIRGINIA

fiddles

FRANKFORT ✱   ● LEXINGTON

coal mining

THE KNOBS

● LOUISVILLE

Churchill Downs race track

INDIANA

OHIO RIVER

Daniel Boone National Forest

farming

● OWENSBORO

Mammoth Cave

BOWLING GREEN ●

ILLINOIS

great blue herons

LAND OF TEN THOUSAND SINKS

TENNESSEE

Mammoth Cave

Explore underground at this World Heritage Site. The cave leads to lakes, rivers, and more than 350 miles (560 km) of passageways.

● PADUCAH

MISSISSIPPI RIVER

MISSOURI

Daniel Boone National Forest

Picnic, hike, camp, and fish in this rugged area of the Appalachian Mountains. There are forests, sandstone cliffs, rivers, and streams here.

TENNESSEE

This wide state has many different areas.
The Great Smoky Mountains, busy cities,
and cotton farms are all found here.
The cities are growing quickly, and the state
is important in the country music industry.

Great Smoky Mountains National Park

Visit one of the most popular national parks in the country. At the beginning of summer, a rare type of firefly lives here that all blink at the same time!

VIRGINIA

KINGSPORT

UNAKA MOUNTAINS

Dollywood

KNOXVILLE

Dollywood theme park

NORTH CAROLINA

spruce trees

Great Smoky Mountains

KENTUCKY

TENNESSEE RIVER

GREAT APPALACHIAN VALLEY

GEORGIA

Grand Ole Opry
✳ NASHVILLE

CUMBERLAND PLATEAU

CHATTANOOGA

maple trees

cotton farming

corn

ALABAMA

Grand Ole Opry

Watch a performance at one of the country's best theaters. The Opry began as a radio show in 1925, and now musicians of all genres perform here.

MISSOURI

TENNESSEE RIVER

MISSISSIPPI RIVER

great blue herons

bobcats

N

ARKANSAS

Graceland
● MEMPHIS

Graceland

Tour the home of Elvis Presley, one of rock and roll's greatest stars. You can even board one of his personal airplanes!

FAST FACTS

Size: 42,144 square miles (109,152 km²)
Population: 6.7 million
Joined the Union: June 1, 1796
State nickname: Volunteer State
State bird: Northern mockingbird

MISSISSIPPI

Home to the famous Mississippi River, this small state has a name that means "great waters" or "father of waters." Mississippi is the birthplace of blues music. In the past, this state was home to many rural plantations.

TENNESSEE

ARKANSAS

TUPELO

B. B. King Museum

chickens

BLACK PRAIRIE

tornadoes

harp music

MERIDIAN

Vicksburg National Military Park

JACKSON

Piney Woods

CENTRAL PRAIRIE

ALABAMA

MISSISSIPPI RIVER

wild turkeys

magnolia flowers

HATTIESBURG

LOUISIANA

shrimp

GULFPORT   BILOXI

SHIP ISLAND

Vicksburg National Military Park

Learn about the Civil War at this battleground which is the final resting place for 17,000 soldiers.

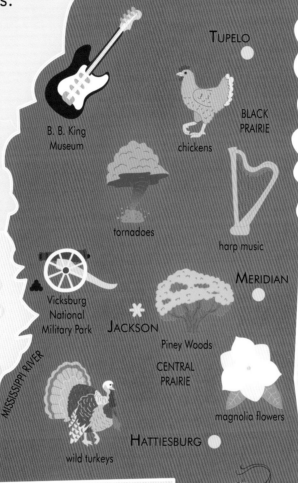

B.B. King Museum

Listen to the blues, study its history, and learn about B.B. King, the man who spread blues music around the world.

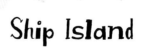

Size: 48,411 square miles (125,384 km²)

Population: 3 million

Joined the Union: December 10, 1817

State nickname: Magnolia State

State bird: Northern mockingbird

Ship Island

Look for sea shells, admire dolphins, and play on the beach. This protected island is a quick ferry ride away from the mainland.

ALABAMA

This southern state is shaped like a rectangle and includes many different types of land. There are rugged forests in the mountains and vast plains by the Gulf coast. Much of the Civil War and the civil rights movement was fought here.

U.S. Space and Rocket Center

Attend Space Camp and learn about America's history in space. This is the second-biggest research park in the country.

Dismals Canyon Conservatory

Visit at night to see the glow worms light up. This natural landmark is located deep in the Appalachian Mountains.

TENNESSEE

MISSISSIPPI

U.S. Space and Rocket Center

HUNTSVILLE

TENNESSEE RIVER

APPALACHIAN MOUNTAINS

Dismals Canyon Conservatory

CUMBERLAND PLATEAU

peanuts

pine trees

BIRMINGHAM

TUSCALOOSA

yellow-shafted flickers

PIEDMONT PLATEAU

opossums

MONTGOMERY

alligators

CHATTAHOOCHEE RIVER

GEORGIA

farming

cotton farming

MOBILE

FLORIDA

N

FAST FACTS

Size: 52,419 square miles (135,765 km²)

Population: 4.9 million

Joined the Union: December 14, 1819

State nickname: Cotton State

State bird: Yellowhammer

OHIO

Ohio lies on the eastern edge of the Midwest. It was once a rural state but is now one of the most populated states in the country. Astronaut Neil Armstrong lived in Ohio.

Rock and Roll Hall of Fame and Museum

Learn about the history of music. The hall of fame displays items from some of the world's greatest performers.

MICHIGAN

LAKE ERIE

Cleveland Museum of Art

CLEVELAND

YOUNGSTOWN

TOLEDO

Cuyahoga National Park

Rock and Roll Hall of Fame and Museum

AKRON

white-tailed deer

WABASH RIVER

Amish buggy

groundhogs

INDIANA

COLUMBUS

factories

coal mining

DAYTON

corn

N

CINCINNATI

OHIO RIVER

buckeye trees

PENNSYLVANIA

Cuyahoga National Park

Hike past waterfalls and impressive rock formations. There are 160 miles (257 km) of trails in this park.

WEST VIRGINIA

FAST FACTS

Size: 44,826 square miles (116,099 km^2)

Population: 11.7 million

Joined the Union: March 1, 1803

State nickname: Buckeye State

State bird: Northern cardinal

Cleveland Museum of Art

Enjoy ancient and modern art at this world-class museum. It's home to everything from Monet's paintings of water lilies to Rodin's famous sculpture, called "The Thinker."

WEST VIRGINIA

This small, rugged state is part of the Appalachian Mountains and is the highest state east of the Mississippi River. More than three-quarters of the state is forest and most of the people live in rural areas. Many people here work in the coal mining industry.

Bluestone River Gorge

Enjoy a beautiful view as you travel by aerial tramway. There's also an amphitheater and a craft center in the Pipestem Resort State Park, located within the gorge.

PENNSYLVANIA

MARYLAND

MORGANTOWN

apples

oak trees

OHIO

PARKERSBURG

N

OHIO RIVER

black bears

Monongahela National Forest

CHARLESTOWN

APPALACHIAN MOUNTAINS

GAULEY RIVER

HUNTINGTON

NEW RIVER

KENTUCKY

rabbits

BECKLEY

white water rafting

BLUESTONE RIVER GORGE

National Coal Heritage Area

VIRGINIA

Monongahela National Forest

Visit a bog where cranberries grow, then hike up to Spruce Knob, the highest point in the state. There are over 800 miles (1,200 km) of trails to explore.

Gauley River

Go whitewater rafting in some of the most adventurous waters in the country.

FAST FACTS

Size: 24,230 square miles (62,755 km^2)

Population: 1.8 million

Joined the Union: June 20, 1863

State nickname: Mountain State

State bird: Northern cardinal

VIRGINIA

One of the original 13 colonies, Virginia was home to some of the first Europeans in America and later allowed some of its land to become the U.S. capital, Washington, D.C. The land is filled with lots of historical landmarks and four of the first five presidents were born here.

MARYLAND

CHESAPEAKE BAY

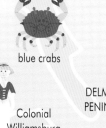
blue crabs

N

ALEXANDRIA

WASHINGTON, D.C.

foxes

RICHMOND *

Colonial Williamsburg

DELMARVA PENINSULA

VIRGINIA BEACH
NORFOLK
CHESAPEAKE

Monticello

Great Dismal Swamp

Shenandoah National Park

opossums

ROANOKE RIVER

coal mining

Monticello

Tour the home of President Thomas Jefferson and learn what life was like in the 1700s. This is now a World Heritage Site.

WEST VIRGINIA

GREAT APPALACHIAN VALLEY

black bears

BLUE RIDGE MOUNTAINS

CLINCH RIVER

KENTUCKY

pine trees

NORTH CAROLINA

Colonial Williamsburg

Travel back in time to see what life was like in the colonies. This is the world's largest living history museum.

FAST FACTS

Size: 42,775 square miles (110,787 km²)
Population: 8.5 million
Joined the Union: June 25, 1788
State nickname: Mother of Presidents
State bird: Northern cardinal

Shenandoah National Park

Enjoy waterfalls, quiet woods, and spectacular views. This national park is just 75 miles (120 km) away from Washington, D.C., but feels hidden and wild.

Size: 53,819 square miles (139,391 km^2)

Population: 10 million

Joined the Union: November 21, 1789

State nickname: Old North State

State bird: Northern cardinal

Cape Hatteras Lighthouse

Climb the 257 stairs in the country's tallest lighthouse, also known as "America's Lighthouse."

Wild Horses

Visit the Outer Banks islands to admire some of the country's only wild horses. It's a rare and beautiful sight to see them running on the beach.

VIRGINIA

OUTER BANKS

wild horses

ROANOKE ISLAND

red spruce trees

CHOWAN RIVER

Cape Hatteras

DURHAM

★ RALEIGH

fiddles

GREENSBORO

LOOKOUT CAPE

sweet potatoes

chickens

THE COASTAL PLAIN

N

Mount Mitchell

FAYETTEVILLE

THE PIEDMONT

rabbits

WILMINGTON

TENNESSEE

raccoons

CHARLOTTE

Venus flytraps

ASHEVILLE

Triple Falls

SOUTH CAROLINA

NORTH CAROLINA

GEORGIA

Triple Falls

Grab your camera. This three-tiered waterfall in Brevard is a state favorite. There are over 350 waterfalls in this state.

Roanoke Island, part of North Carolina, was the place where early colonists first landed in 1587. The first settlers didn't survive, but later North Carolina became one of the original 13 colonies. It is one of the wettest states in the country and home to many marshlands and lakes.

SOUTH CAROLINA

South Carolina was one of the original 13 colonies. It is known for its subtropical beaches and college football teams. The captial city, Columbia, is named for Italian explorer Christopher Columbus. The first battle of the Civil War took place here.

Hilton Head

Relax on this island resort. There are many restaurants, tennis courts, and golf courses.

SASSAFRAS MOUNTAIN

BLUE RIDGE MOUNTAINS

GREENVILLE

football

PIEDMONT PROVINCE

nuclear power

COLUMBIA

GEORGIA

SAVANNAH RIVER

cotton farming

white-tailed deer

NORTH CAROLINA

GREAT PEE DEE RIVER

beavers

tornadoes

MYRTLE BEACH

SANTEE RIVER

COASTAL PLAIN

Boone Hall plantation

CHARLESTON

fiddles

Spoleto Festival

SEA ISLANDS

Hilton Head

N

Spoleto Festival

Enjoy the dramatic performances at this annual event. There are actors, dancers, singers, musicians, and artists.

Boone Hall Plantation

Walk down the Avenue of the Oaks to visit one of the most famous plantations in the world. You can also visit nine original slave cabins and learn more about this difficult time in history.

FAST FACTS

Size: 32,020 square miles (82,931 km²)
Population: 5 million
Joined the Union: May 23, 1788
State nickname: Palmetto State
State bird: Carolina wren

FLORIDA

Florida has a long coastline as well as many swamps. The land and its sunny weather have made this state a popular place to live or visit as a tourist. The weather also means that Florida produces more citrus fruits, such as lemons and oranges, than any other state.

Walt Disney World

Find some magic in this world-famous theme park. You can meet your favorite Disney characters and go on exciting rides.

Castillo de San Marcos

Learn what life was like in the 1600s at this national monument. It's one of the oldest forts in the country and is in the shape of a star.

N

PENSACOLA

white ibis

TALLAHASSEE

APALACHICOLA RIVER

sunshine

GULF OF MEXICO

manatees

JACKSONVILLE

Castillo de San Marcos

palm trees

FAST FACTS

Size: 65,757 square miles (170,310 km^2)

Population: 21 million

Joined the Union: March 3, 1845

State nickname: Sunshine State

State bird: Northern mockingbird

ATLANTIC OCEAN

CAPE CANAVERAL

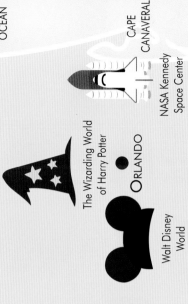

NASA Kennedy Space Center

The Wizarding World of Harry Potter

ORLANDO

Walt Disney World

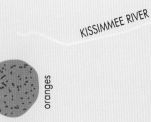

oranges

KISSIMMEE RIVER

LAKE OKEECHOBEE

FORT LAUDERDALE

MIAMI CANAL

CALOOSAHATCHEE RIVER

pumas

MIAMI

The Everglades

golf

NAPLES

TAMPA

SARASOTA

FLORIDA KEYS

hurricanes

The Wizarding World of Harry Potter

Explore Diagon Alley, Hogwarts, and Hogsmeade in this spectacular recreation of the popular series. You can even find a wand at Ollivander's.

NASA Kennedy Space Center

Head to Cape Canaveral to see where rockets are launched. You can even train to be an astronaut on Mars.

Everglades National Park

Look for alligators as you explore the largest subtropical wilderness in the U.S. It's also a World Heritage site.

GEORGIA

Georgia stretches from the Blue Ridge Mountains in the north of the state, to the Atlantic Ocean, but its borders originally included Alabama and Mississippi, too. Slave plantations were once important here. Today many large companies have their headquarters here.

Jekyll Island

Play golf, bike, or swim with dolphins on this beautiful island. It's the southernmost island in the Golden Isles.

NORTH CAROLINA

SOUTH CAROLINA

N

TENNESSEE

SAVANNAH RIVER

AUGUSTA

SAVANNAH

peaches

ALPHARETTA

jazz

ATHENS

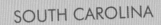
cotton plants

NORTH OCONEE RIVER

pecans

GOLDEN ISLES

dolphins

MARIETTA

CHATTAHOOCHEE RIVER

ATLANTA

World of Coca-Cola

MACON

opossums

alligators

OKEFENOKEE SWAMP

FLORIDA

ALABAMA

National Infantry Museum

peanuts

National Infantry Museum

Study over 200 years of military history. There are war simulators and many fascinating exhibits here.

FAST FACTS

Size: 59,425 square miles (153,910 km²)

Population: 10.5 million

Joined the Union: January 2, 1788

State nickname: Peach State

State bird: Brown thrasher

World of Coca-Cola

Learn the history of soda and see the vault where the secret recipe of Coca-Cola is kept.

50

PENNSYLVANIA

N

BRANDYWINE CREEK

Hagley Museum
and Library

WILMINGTON

Mt. Cuba
Center

NEWARK

MIDDLETOWN

Nemours
Estate

DELAWARE RIVER

pine trees

canoeing

Dover

underground
railroad

raccoons

holly

foxes

MARYLAND

DELAWARE
BAY

NEW
JERSEY

FENWICK
ISLAND

Hagley Museum and Library

Learn about Delaware's history as you explore restored mills, gardens, and a workers' community on the banks of the Brandywine Creek.

Nemours Estate

Tour the 105-room mansion that was once built by wealthy businessman Alfred I. duPont. There are also 300 acres of woodlands and gardens to enjoy.

Mt. Cuba Center

Admire the plants in this beautiful botanical garden. It has been here for more than 80 years.

FAST FACTS

Size: 1,982 square miles (5,133 km²)

Population: 1 million

Joined the Union: December 7, 1787

State nickname: First State

State bird: Blue hen chicken

DELAWARE

Delaware was the first state to sign the Constitution of the United States, in 1787. It is one of the smallest states, but it has lots of people. It's official state dessert is peach pie!

MARYLAND

Maryland is a small state located in the center of America's east coast. Much of the state is wetland. It was one of the original 13 colonies, which became the first states, and it allowed some of its land to become the U.S. capital, Washington, D.C. Today much of its activity is related to the government.

United States Naval Academy

Tour the USNA in Annapolis. After four years of training, students join the Navy or Marine Corp.

N

PENNSYLVANIA

APPALACHIAN MOUNTAINS

APPALACHIAN TRAIL

PIEDMONT PLATEAU

DELAWARE

pine trees

WEST VIRGINIA

riding

FREDERICK

Underground Railroad

jousting

oysters

BALTIMORE

BETHESDA

WASHINGTON, D.C.

ANNAPOLIS
United States Naval Academy

COASTAL PLAIN

orioles

Civil War cannon

blue crabs

POTOMAC RIVER

VIRGINIA

ST. CLEMENTS ISLAND

CHESAPEAKE BAY

ASSATEAGUE ISLAND

Appalachian Trail

Hike across Maryland's 38-mile (61-km) stretch of this famous trail. The whole trail reaches from Maine to Georgia.

FAST FACTS

Size: 12,406 square miles (32,131 km²)

Population: 6 million

Joined the Union: April 28, 1788

State nickname: Free State

State bird: Baltimore oriole

Chesapeake Bay

Sail with thousands of others in this beautiful bay. Maryland is the sailing capital of the world!

NEW JERSEY

One of the original 13 colonies, New Jersey is small and urban, despite its Garden State nickname. It was once home to many farms, but is now one of the most populated states. Many people who live here work in New York or Pennsylvania.

Menlo Park

Explore Thomas Edison's laboratory, where he invented the phonograph for recording and playing sound, and the incandescent light bulb.

HACKENSACK RIVER

HUDSON RIVER

PASSAIC RIVER

Great Falls

● PATERSON

pine trees

APPALACHIAN MOUNTAINS

THE HIGHLANDS

NEWARK ●
● JERSEY CITY
● ELIZABETH TOWN

Menlo Park

riding   PIEDMONT

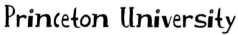

RARITAN RIVER

DELAWARE RIVER

raccoons

Princeton University

✴ TRENTON

Princeton University

Explore the campus of one of America's top universities. James Madison, Michelle Obama, and Jeff Bezos all went here.

azaleas

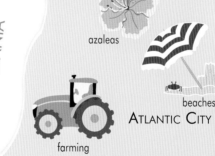

beaches

PENNSYLVANIA

farming

ATLANTIC CITY ●

COASTAL PLAIN

Atlantic City

Enjoy the Atlantic Ocean and the boardwalk in this resort town. You can shop, swim, or relax at a spa here.

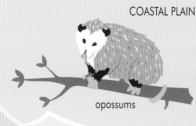

opossums

DELAWARE

FAST FACTS

Size: 8,723 square miles (22,592 km²)
Population: 9 million
Joined the Union: December 18, 1787
State nickname: Garden State
State bird: Eastern goldfinch

PENNSYLVANIA

As one of the original 13 colonies, Pennsylvania played a key role in America's early years. Now it's one of the larger states. The land is rugged, and it took 160 years for the whole state to be settled. Today about half the land is forest.

Groundhog Day

Travel to Punxsutawney to see if a groundhog spots its shadow on February 2nd. This annual tradition is said to tell whether Spring will come early.

Falling Water

Tour this famous house designed by architect Frank Lloyd Wright. It's set over a dramatic waterfall.

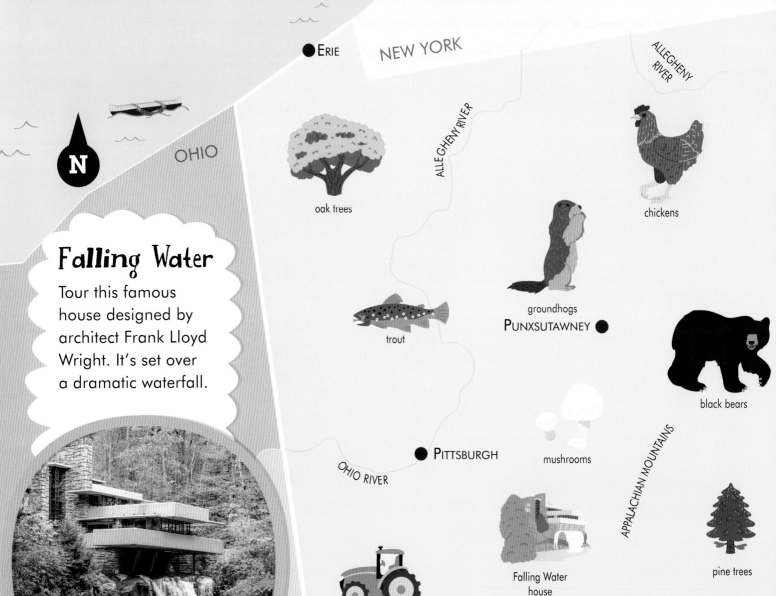

LAKE ERIE

N

OHIO

ERIE

NEW YORK

ALLEGHENY RIVER

ALLEGHENY RIVER

oak trees

chickens

groundhogs

trout

PUNXSUTAWNEY

black bears

PITTSBURGH

mushrooms

OHIO RIVER

APPALACHIAN MOUNTAINS

Falling Water house

pine trees

farming

WEST VIRGINIA

Battle of Gettysburg

Watch a reenactment of one of the Civil War's biggest conflicts. It was fought in Gettysburg in 1863.

NEW YORK

maple trees

● SCRANTON

POCONO MOUNTAINS

white-tailed deer

SUSQUEHANNA RIVER

hex signs

RIDGE AND VALLEY PROVINCE

NEW JERSEY

BETHLEHEM ●
ALLENTOWN ●

DELAWARE RIVER

READING ●

Benjamin Franklin Museum

PHILADELPHIA ●

Battle of Gettysburg

HARRISBURG ✳

LANCASTER ●   Amish

Liberty Bell

pot pie

LANCASTER COUNTY

THE PIEDMONT

DELAWARE

MARYLAND

Lancaster County

Meet the Amish who live according to a traditional understanding of the Bible. You can also eat a traditional Pennsylvania Dutch meal.

Benjamin Franklin Museum

Learn about one of the Founding Fathers of the U.S. at this national historic park. There are objects on display, demonstrations, and interactive exhibits.

MAINE

Located on the Canadian border, Maine is the largest New England state. It has a long, rocky coastline, long winters, and eighty percent of the land is covered with forest. Wild blueberries are the official state fruit of Maine.

CANADA

ST. JOHN RIVER

ALLAGASH RIVER

porcupines

blueberries

MOUNT KATAHDIN

pine trees

APPALACHIAN MOUNTAINS

MOOSEHEAD LAKE

Moxie sodas

moose

KENNEBEC RIVER

BANGOR

ANDROSCOGGIN RIVER

Acadia National Park

BAR HARBOR

CAMDEN HILLS

AUGUSTA

lobsters

salmon

LEWISTON

ROCKPORT

Thompson Ice House

SACO RIVER

PORTLAND

CAPE ELIZABETH

SACO

BIDDEFORD

Rachel Carson National Wildlife Refuge

schooners

BAY OF FUNDY

Acadia National Park

Explore the Bass Harbor Head Lighthouse. This national park features dramatic cliffs right by the water.

Rachel Carson National Wildlife Refuge

Walk through salt marshes and estuaries. A wooden boardwalk makes it easy to enjoy this beautiful wildlife refuge, home to many birds and animals.

The Thompson Ice House

Visit this museum in winter to watch as volunteers harvest ice. They use the same methods that workers did in the 1800s to saw, move, and store the ice.

Size: 35,380 square miles (91,634 km²)

Population: 1.3 million

Joined the Union: March 15, 1820

State nickname: Pine Tree State

State bird: Black-capped chickadee

VERMONT

Vermont lies on the Canadian border. This New England state is home to many trees but not many residents. Lots of people live and work in other states for the majority of the year, but they enjoy spending their holidays in Vermont. The state is known for its beautiful landscape.

Stowe Recreation Path

Walk, bike, ski, or horseback ride along this 5-mile paved trail. It winds along a river and ends in Stowe Village, where you can eat lunch or visit a bookstore.

CANADA

NEW YORK

MISSISQUOI RIVER

LAKE CHAMPLAIN

N

pine trees

skiing

maple trees

GREEN MOUNTAINS

moose

COLCHESTER

STOWE RECREATION PATH

BURLINGTON   ESSEX   STOWE

WINOOSKI RIVER

SHELBURNE   SOUTH
               BURLINGTON   maple syrup

Shelburne Farms   * MONTPELIER

CHAMPLAIN VALLEY

cows

RUTLAND

New England
falconry

CONNECTICUT RIVER

NEW HAMPSHIRE

covered bridges

white-tailed deer

DOVER

Shelburne Farms

Tour a working farm, sample cheese, and hike up the hills to enjoy a view of Lake Champlain. This is a National Historic Landmark.

New England Falconry

Fly a hawk, watch a hunt, and explore the forest as you learn about the ancient practice of falconry.

FAST FACTS

Size: 9,616 square miles (24,905 km^2)

Population: 0.6 million

Joined the Union: March 4, 1791

State nickname: Green Mountain State

State bird: Hermit thrush

NEW HAMPSHIRE

Touching the Canadian border and Massachusetts, New Hampshire is a long state. It is one of the original 13 colonies and has strong ties to the nation's history. The state has lots of industries but also has large areas of open land. New Hampshire is known for its small, pretty towns.

Franconia Notch State Park

Hike to the Flume Gorge in the heart of the White Mountains. You'll find impressive waterfalls and scenic views in this natural chasm.

Ice Castles

Wander through the icy structures that are built each winter. It's a cold but memorable experience.

N

moose

Franconia Notch State Park

WHITE MOUNTAINS

Old Man of the Mountain

ice castles

MAINE

VERMONT

CONNECTICUT RIVER

LAKE WINNIPESAUKEE

CANTERBURY SHAKER VILLAGE

Shaker art

ROCHESTER

DOVER

lobsters

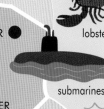

submarines

*CONCORD

MERRIMACK RIVER

MANCHESTER

SALEM

MERRIMACK

NASHUA

KEENE

white-tailed deer

MASSACHUSETTS

Canterbury Shaker Village

Learn about Shaker life at this preserved village. The religious community was active here from 1792–1992.

Walden Pond

Walk around the pond that Henry David Thoreau wrote about. You can also peek inside the small cottage he lived in.

MASSACHUSETTS

This small New England state was one of the original 13 colonies. The Revolutionary War against the British was started here. Today it is a modern state with a diverse population in Boston and rural towns in the western half of the state.

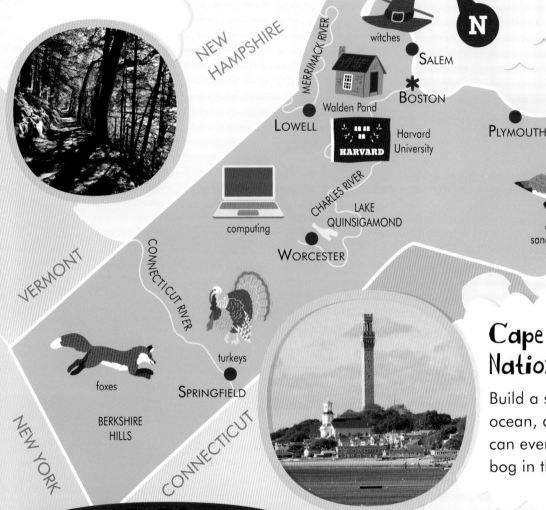

MAINE

NEW HAMPSHIRE

MERRIMACK RIVER

witches

N

SALEM

cranberries

BOSTON

Walden Pond

LOWELL

Cape Cod

HARVARD

Harvard University

PLYMOUTH

CHARLES RIVER

LAKE QUINSIGAMOND

NANTUCKET ISLAND

lobsters

computing

WORCESTER

sandpipers

MARTHA'S VINEYARD

VERMONT

CONNECTICUT RIVER

turkeys

foxes

SPRINGFIELD

BERKSHIRE HILLS

NEW YORK

CONNECTICUT

Cape Cod National Seashore

Build a sandcastle, swim in the ocean, and tour a lighthouse. You can even explore a wild cranberry bog in this national park.

FAST FACTS

Size: 10,565 square miles (27,363 km^2)

Population: 7 million

Joined the Union: February 6, 1788

State nickname: Bay State

State bird: Black-capped chickadee

Freedom Trail

Follow this famous path through Boston. As you walk, you'll see Boston Common and Paul Revere's house.

CONNECTICUT

One of the original 13 colonies, Connecticut has a mix of urban areas, beaches, and historic sites. Most of this small New England state is wooded. In other areas it has lots of people and successful businesses.

Mark Twain House

Tour the Hartford house where the writer of *Adventures of Huckleberry Finn*, Mark Twain, lived.

MASSACHUSETTS

RHODE ISLAND

BERKSHIRE HILLS

APPALACHIAN MOUNTAINS

fall leaves

* HARTFORD

Mark Twain House

oak trees

WATERBURY

LAKE CANDLEWOOD

HOUSATONIC RIVER

CONNECTICUT RIVER

turkeys

Putnam Memorial State Park

NEW HAVEN

Grace Farms

BRIDGEPORT

oysters

bluefish

STAMFORD

LONG ISLAND SOUND

Grace Farms

Wander the grounds at this beautiful site. It's a church, farm, school, library, basketball court, and tea garden all rolled into one.

Putnam Memorial State Park

See where the Continental Army camped in 1779 during the Revolutionary War. There's a reconstructed log building and a museum.

RHODE ISLAND

This tiny state is one of the original 13 colonies. It is densely populated and has more than 400 miles (640 km) of coastline. In the 18th century, large mansions were built on the coast, which can now be toured. With so many resort areas, this state has been called "the playground of New England."

The Breakers

Tour this enormous mansion. It was once a summer "cottage" for the Vanderbilt family.

Rhode Island School of Design

See the work of students and world-famous artists at this museum and college.

MASSACHUSETTS

CONNECTICUT

BLACKSTONE RIVER

trumpets

PAWTUCKET

PROVIDENCE

coyotes

PAWTUXET RIVER

Rhode Island School of Design

CRANSTON

WARWICK

MOUNT HOPE BAY

clams

NARRAGANSETT BAY

spruce trees

books

foxes

diamond rings

lobsters

The Breakers

PAWCATUCK RIVER

Cliff Walk

yachting

BLOCK ISLAND

Cliff Walk

Walk along the eastern shore of Rhode Island. These rocky cliffs feature wildflowers, stunning architecture, and a great view of the ocean.

NEW YORK

One of the original 13 colonies, New York state borders Canada and is well-known as the home of New York City. The Statue of Liberty in the city was a gift to the United States from France. The state was originally named New Netherlands by Dutch settlers.

Strong National Museum of Play

See the world's largest collection of toys. The museum was made to get visitors of all ages to play.

LAKE ONTARIO

ERIE CANAL

ROCHESTER

Strong National Museum of Play

Niagara Falls

BUFFALO

chickens

SYRACUSE

squirrels

rabbits

FINGER LAKES

CHEMUNG RIVER

fox

ALLEGHENY RIVER

PENNSYLVANIA

Niagara Falls

Admire the waterfall at the nation's oldest state park. It lies on the Canadian border.

Central Park

Eat a hot dog, watch a street performer, or look up at the amazing skyscrapers. It's all possible in Manhattan's famous park.

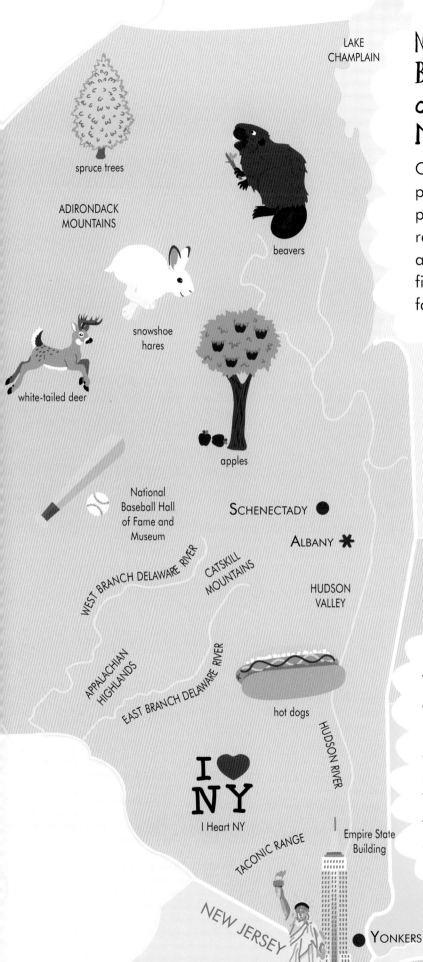

LAKE CHAMPLAIN

spruce trees

ADIRONDACK MOUNTAINS

beavers

snowshoe hares

white-tailed deer

apples

National Baseball Hall of Fame and Museum

SCHENECTADY ●

ALBANY ✳

WEST BRANCH DELAWARE RIVER

CATSKILL MOUNTAINS

HUDSON VALLEY

APPALACHIAN HIGHLANDS

EAST BRANCH DELAWARE RIVER

hot dogs

HUDSON RIVER

I ♥ NY
I Heart NY

TACONIC RANGE

Empire State Building

NEW JERSEY

Statue of Liberty

YONKERS ●

NEW YORK CITY ●

Metropolitan Museum of Art

MASSACHUSETTS

National Baseball Hall of Fame and Museum

Celebrate America's pastime where the best players in history are remembered. There are artifacts and a baseball field where hall of famers play.

FAST FACTS

Size: 54,556 square miles (141,299 km^2)

Population: 20 million

Joined the Union: July 26, 1788

State nickname: Empire State

State bird: Eastern bluebird

Metropolitan Museum of Art

Explore galleries that cover more than 5,000 years of art. You'll find everything from Egyptian tombs to abstract paintings here.

INDEX